Living the Abundant Life

Words of Wisdom from a Rich-man

Gary W. Richman, Ph.D.

Acknowledgements

I would first off like to acknowledge the Universe for its help and guidance. There are many high school counselors who would be shocked to learn that this dyslexic, reading disordered, less than mediocre student has written another book let alone one. The next thanks must go to my editor Gretchen Kvistad who not only helps with my grammar and word usage, but keeps the focus of the book consistent with my goals and tone. I am truly indebted to you for your skills and respectful collaboration. I could not have been more fortunate than when she came to help me.

I would like to acknowledge Georgia Deaver for her brillant cover illustrations. Also I would like to thank her for being patient with someone whose ability to visualize abstracts is challenged.

We all would like our parents to honor us with their sense of pride in what we do. I would like to thank my mother for hers. One is never too old to hear such important things.

I would like to acknowledge the long term friends I have who have always honored me with their respect, honesty, and caring. These people know who they are. You have all been so valuable and important when things have gone well, and more importantly not so well.

I would like to acknowledge my wife, Lisa. Though we are the mirror to each others growth, which can be trying, she stays the course. She supports and encourages my work as not only a priority, but as important. She is a light of energy and power that is unequaled in most circles, and lets me know even in the difficult times that I am loved.

Preface

As we attend to classes, seminars, lectures, or even sitting at the feet of an incarnate, we may not feel that this is the vehicle we were hoping would open up our minds. We keep wandering through different aspects of the same message looking for that ah ha resonance that gets not only our attention, but grabs our life like never before and won't let us go. This resounding resonance is so loud that we know our lives have been changed forever. Now that is a tall order and am I so presumptuous that I believe this will happen to you as you ponder what I have to say? No never presumptuous, hopeful. Why? Because to be the facilitator of your opening to a different and more compete you is my goal.

This book is a culmination of a life time of working on my own spiritual practices and walking my path. It is completely derived from a stream of conscious that over a couple of years kept coming into consciousness and manifesting on paper. It is not that these are new or never heard of intentions or ponderings, but my approach to age old ways of living life in a peaceful, empowered, and centered manner. As I say to my patients, you can have many instructors teaching anything from skiing to dance, but it may never seem to gel. The gelling can only occur when it is put to you in the way that completely resonates and can therefore be deeply internalized. My aim in life is to be that swizzle stick that melds all the juices of the formula called you culminating in the best and zestiest blend of your truest and divine self.

To understand the immense power of our ability to intention abundance, sit and truly ponder the oh so true quote: As You Believe It, So Is It Done Unto You.

Listening to our inner voice is as easy as sitting in the silence between words. It is the surrendering to all we were taught to pay attention to and value, while being face to face with ourselves without distraction or our subconscious learned miss-beliefs.

If we could truly remember that we are souls having human experiences, then we could embrace the soul in each of us and ask the human what he/she learned today.

Whether you walk the Taoist, Buddhist, Judea/Christian, Hindu, Native American, or Spiritual path, they all start with the same first step: Surrender the *insecurities and competitiveness* of the ego for the inner truth of the divine self.

To internalize that we are all souls having human experiences means we are all family of the Universe. Once we accept that, then our task is to enhance our own growth and not to *judge or compete* with family.

Mindfulness is one of the most important spiritual practices that there is. It is essential to truly seeing all that the Universe is, and to live in the moment as a part of the One.

People often say that when disaster comes you had better have you own supplies, but the truth of the matter is that at such times egos take a back seat while souls step up to help their fellow human beings.

Courage is not the absence of fear, but taking action or stretching beyond your self in spite of it.

To live from the inside out is the empowered path. Only then can you enhance the aura of truth that is the totality of you.

To be empowered and to be in truth, one must come from an open hearted place of all that one is.

To be alive and walk free one must feel all that is from Mother Earth and Father Sky, and the energetic beings therein.

To be in the community of light-minded beings expands my energy, opens my heart and makes me smile. I am honored to be among you.

To walk in the openness of your heart and your truth offers the depth of vulnerability necessary to claim your divine empowerment.

Carrying out ones spiritual practices, like walking ones path is not always easy, but with discipline and tenacity the results are always glorious.

Miracles happen every day. The unconscious ignores it, and rationalizes this as luck or coincidence, while the mindful, enlightened ones stand in gratitude.

Is there anything more deeply profound then sitting in the quiet of your own being and experiencing the peaceful bliss of the Universe?

Are you a human doing or a human being? To be or not to be, now there *is* a question.

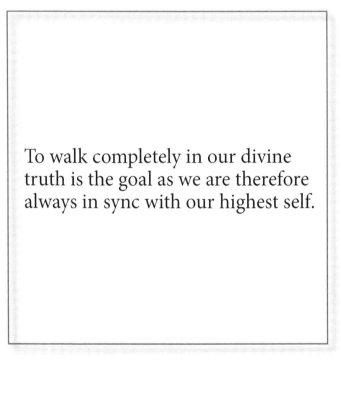

To walk completely in our divine truth is the goal as we are therefore always in sync with our highest self.

The more we surrender our beliefs of who we think we are, the deeper is the relationship to our inherent nature.

The more we can mitigate our subconscious miss-beliefs of self, the deeper our connection to our own divinity.

When the ego arrives at the place of not knowing who it is or what is so, it is then that we are on the verge of wisdom.

Whenever you get to the most impatient and frustrated place in your life and yell out, what is it I am suppose to get from this? Remember not only will the answer come, but it is always geared toward *mindfulness, consciousness, and wisdom.*

It is in silence between the breaths
where we truly find our divine self.

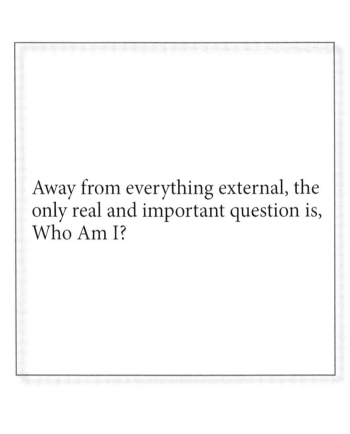

Away from everything external, the only real and important question is, Who Am I?

The old clichés and quotes still have the right stuff; Is there any more important inner work to be accomplished than that of the Shakespearean quote: To Thine Own Self Be True?

I believe that unconditional love is the juice that holds the Universe together. Recognizing that each soul is working out his/her lessons on this earth allows you to have respect and compassion for each person's quest.

As I often say, enlightenment is easy; dismantling and surrendering our egoic programming is a lifelong task.

Only the unconscious believe in coincidences. Those who are seeking awareness pay attention to all actions as they are lessons designed to bring you closer to your self and the Universe/God.

To have the courage to go into your shadow world and ferret out the false demons is the important work of healing your inner child, and reclaiming your inherent nature.

It is so sad that due to narrow thinking and fear, people see different as bad instead of just an alternative expression of the divine.

To come from truth is the easiest way to walk life, as there is only one truth devoid of ego; solid and divine.

What is this yearning that sets light beings apart and keeps them walking the spiritual path; persisting without logic or tangible manifestations; yet staying in the hunt?

All that comes to us has to do with owning yourself from the inside out. As you respect, honor, own your rights in this life, and love yourself, so to will it be done unto you. Expecting it to come to you "just because" while adding $3.50 will get you coffee.

Due to our indoctrination by Western society's way of looking outside of ones self for validation and recognition, we think to look out rather than in to remember and reclaim who we truly are.

As we, through insight and consciousness, dismantle the walls/
armor/ego defenses that have safe-
guarded us always, we begin to
venture back to the divine child
within, reminding us that we are
magnificent.

To find our way back to our true inner nature, beneath the ego is our path to all that is important with regard to self mastery.

When we do not have the desire and the courage to look at our shadow side and explore our feelings, we act them out. Therefore, it hurts to feel and work through our issues, but if we do not process these feelings, the acting out that will ensue will blow up our lives.

Gerry Jampolsky wrote the opposite of love is fear. I tell my patients that you cannot live in fear and faith. If you are in fear you are constricted, seeking to hide and be safe, not really living just not dying. If we live in love and faith, we live an expanded life of courage and growth, learning our lessons and empowering and remembering our divine self.

Loving unconditionally does not mean you accept every act, perspective, or behavior of someone you love; it means you accept them completely at the core/soul level of their divine self.

Your intellect is a great computer to make tangible our wants, desires, intentions, goals, passions, and hopes. All too often we think it is the intellect and mind by them-selves that are the deal, and we forget to remember where it all originates from, i.e., our heartfelt inner self.

Real friendship is one in which someone has your back, holds your confidence, has earned your trust, you can say what you need to without being judged, and be completely your self with. All others are acquaintances and strangers.

To walk toward our inner divine nature takes great courage, as we must cross the threshold of our shadow, housing our deepest (miss) fears of self.

To walk between the all and nothing, hence the extremes of life, are where all the options are, and where all the answers can be found.

Understanding all of who we are, what we want, desire, intention, and seek is derived from the heart (the hardware). The head is just the computer to make it tangible (the software).

If your goal is to go deeper into the passions and gifts that are yours, you must do the deeper insight work required to get out of your own way. Good mining is about digging, not walking around the perimeter hoping to find a precious stone.

To value your own counsel and to validate your own wisdom is a necessary strong step to personal acknowledgement that you are a credible person, worth relying on. If you don't know it why should anyone else?

Divine love emanates from your heart and soul. It is not of the personality, but of the spirit of oneness that goes beyond ego and embraces the totality of all that someone is.

How do we handle change? It was an error to say that the only two things we can count on are death and taxes. Change is as sure as the sun coming up in the morning. Do you fight change, which is going against the Tao, or do you embrace the challenge and bring all of your self to embrace it?

How often do you find yourself using the word, trying? I tried to do this, I am trying to be that, or I tried talking to him/her. Trying is the language of failure. The fact is we either do or don't do. If you have been trying for a long time around anything, you might want to look at your deeper intention.

Many of us have been raised with the word love surrounding statements of judgment, control, denigration, and expectation. We then learn to believe that this is love, while in reality it is judgment and negativity. We then find others to love us in this way, while believing we are the one who is wrong or not enough.

Deepening into the spiritual path is in essence eroding more of your miss-beliefs and dismantling mitigating your ego. As this takes you further into your divine self, you take on a demeanor of oneness, which has no judgment or evaluation; hence becoming the witness *living* in a state of grace and love as you experience your path.

When you find that someone who has caused you to feel rage or hate, you might want to thank them for putting you back in touch with that which you still have to work on.

To truly grasp the impermanence of life allows you to be truly present while treasuring every moment.

To truly forgive someone means you must understand deep in your feelings, how what they did affected you. To merely forgive because it is the "right" thing to do cheapens the reality of what happened and what you are forgiving them for. In this way it allows you both to heal.

As you believe it, so is it done unto you. How many of us have heard this and passed it off as just another biblical quote? The truth is Quantum Physics, Metaphysics, Transpersonal Psychology, and Eastern Philosophy all concur that we create our own realty on a daily basis. Our conscious and subconscious verbal and intentioned messaging are impacting what does or does not manifest in our lives. *Think about it.*

Love in the Christ or spiritual consciousness is not really a feeling, but
a state of grace that has no room for
ego, judgment, or anything other
than unconditional acceptance of
all souls as they pursue their lessons
on this school ground called earth.

What is it I do not own when I won't let go of the past? Is it my negative identity or is it that I won't allow myself to step into greatness? If I hold onto that which makes me less, how can I possible embrace my highest self? Is it as Marianne Williamson said, "that our deepest fear is that we are powerful beyond measure?" Therefore, living in the past with our negativity would certainly ensure that.

Mindfulness, and dismissing negative thoughts are the trick to living in joy. Only when we stay away from the glass half empty and fill our selves with positive conscious intention, will we feel passion and contentment. It is not about ignoring life's difficult/ negative issues, but it is also not about letting it define us.

As I center and firmly walk from my core sense of self, they may shoot arrows but they find no target. As I walk empowered from within, I am impervious to attack.

The egoic nature needs to judge and compete, because it never has a sense of worth or value. It only knows what it wants to be, and never is. When we surrender the unconscious/subconscious miss-beliefs manifested through the ego, we then remember that we are divine souls of the Universe. Then there is no need to win approval, only to love and enjoy the incredible being that we are.

Every reaction to our world is due to our script/story. It is our learned personality that harbors the wounds at the root of who we were taught to be. Once we do this, we are able to learn what needs healing and not let it ruin us. We are free to invest in different, healthier options. As we change the roots of a tree, so does the tree change.

The purpose of psychotherapy
is not to blame or pawn off respon-
sibility of your inner work onto
others. It is to understand that the
origins of the self-pollutants infect-
ing your unconscious/subconscious
are not yours. Your job however
is to work through these self-
denigrating toxins, ridding yourself
of them so that your healthier self
can emerge.

A personally tough day is an opportunity to go inside, breath, and do the work necessary to clean house. Too often we look outside ourselves for the origin of the problem, which is not where the problem lies. It takes courage to do the internal work, but oh so rewarding for one's personal empowerment.

Everything that goes on from life experiences to each person who crosses your path is an opportunity to engage in your lessons. These lessons point to what you still have to work on to rid yourself of unwanted unconscious/subconscious data contributing to insecurities, fear and poor behavior, which impede the connection to your true self and the divine.

To be in a constant state of love is to accept that we are all doing our best even when it's dysfunctional. As the Dalai Lama forgives the Chinese for their indiscretions, so too must we realize that it is all the grand illusion of the Universal play being acted out for our growth and advancement.

I have had a discussion with a Buddhist monk on face book who told me that to invite anyone to walk back into their divine self is folly, as there has never been and never will be a self. In the ultimate world of the Buddhist nature he is correct, however I invited him to consider that most of us in the West are a long way from that, and finding our highest and truest self is a necessary, wonderful, and joyous first step.

Who are we, is often the question of the day. However, where do you go to answer this? Like most people do you look outside your self for such validation? To friends, enemies, stereotypes, credibly accepted milestones, societal baselines or fashionably touted accoutrement? Or do you look to the only true place where such an answer could be found, i.e., inside.

I keep hearing a saying that I thought I would like to post: Yesterday is history, tomorrow is a mystery and today is a gift called the present. Wouldn't it be neat to hold each day as gift that you unwrap and enjoy with no garbage from the past or anxiety about the future?

There is an energetic of knowing where true bliss and contentment couple with the Universe. In this state there is a harmony and a dance in which there is a peaceful inner acceptance that everything is OK. This originates from a feeling place, not theory. To the extent that you do not own this perspective, you can see that you have been in your own way, intentioning less than abundance.

Striving for the true energetic of abundance and joy is the goal. What is interesting is that unlike more tangible processes, it is not the looking or the striving, but actually creating the space to internalize the energetic that is the deal. As you surrender that which is in your way, the energetic finds you.

People believe that wisdom and consciousness are achieved by learning more. In actuality, it is accomplished by surrendering to being less, a la becoming nothing. It is the unlearning of who we think and have been taught to believe we are that must reversed.

I have always felt and I have taught others that faith and friendship show up in the hard times, not the easy ones. As all of us face moments of hard times, how true are you to your faith and where are your friends. In such moments we get to see what's so.

The moment we begin to doubt or fall into our fears is the moment that the Universe gets the signal that we want to back off from goodness and abundance, and it accommodates.

To be able to walk into the infinite and become apart of the quantum whole is the goal. One merges into the complete nothingness that is the essence of being in the divine. To merge at this level is peaceful, expanded, and in bliss of the all.

When life is seemingly out of control and you are wondering why you are out of sorts, or "all over the place," re-center. It is often the case that you are not grounded and need an energetic realignment.

Change is an absolute. Yet we are so frightened of change, we restrict and constrict ourselves into cringing, small beings hanging onto stagnation. And yet we wonder why our intentions are not being fulfilled.

How many times have we heard the biblical quote, 'Ye though I walk through the shadow of Death, I fear no evil as thy rod and thy staff accompany me.' And yet how many of us carry that faith and knowing with us as we walk this path called life? Do you carry your faith with you knowing that you are looked after and protected? Do you intention and put your attention on this?

The essence of the love we imagine
and think of as God's love is beyond
our conceptual understanding. It
is due to the immensity of the bliss
and acceptance that is the divine.
It is for us to love fully and truly
climbing the heights to mimic the
divine.

The mind/body continuum is not a misnomer. If your body is diagnosed with something and you check out what this part of the body represents to the mind or the emotional plane, you will see why the dis-ease occurred. The illness is real and must be attended to, but don't forget to also attend to the lesson your body is attempting to get your attention about.

So many people parallel having things with enhancing their self worth/ego. Too many others believe that to pursue personal nothingness involves not owning/having any-thing. The bottom line is to give up identifying the ego as self, and step into the nothingness of true self that is the divinity of everything.

What you own and toys you have are just stuff, enjoy them as that.

Why has intentioning and the discussion of this dimmed? It is my impression that too many people wanted what they wanted for the wrong reasons and intentioned from the wrong place. Intentioning is a high level visual energetic that comes from a pure place of desire and want for the highest good. It is neither egoic nor intellectual, but rather a connection from the highest source.

We need to let go of our over inflated self/ego and get out of our way. Our intellect has studied a lot, but it is not the seat of knowing. That place is in the deeper levels of our true and divine self. It is the place where truth resonates and epiphanies exist.

In the Western world much of life is about fear and restriction. Spiritual journeys are about expanding and being generous whether it involves tithing or being in service.

The more we reach out and stretch the more the Universe meets us with abundance.

As the saying goes, Man makes plans and God just laughs. Often when the "right" opportunity came or a miracle happened, we were in a moment of not caring or letting "it" go. And guess what, "it" just happened. This is not coincidence or luck, but the Universe at work. Let go, let God, and the river a la the Tao just flows.

To conquer our fear and judgments is our human assignment, while *reclaiming* our truth is and being empowered is the reward.

How do you hold your faith when all around you people seem to be losing theirs? Well, that is the time when it is most important to hold tight to what you know and believe in. It is our faith in knowing that the right thing is going on for the right reason that allows us to be strong. From this place of faith and patience, we are given over time the proof that this is so and correct.

The ego fights to hold onto who it should be, having been taught that our true self could never be enough. When the self surrenders its "bloated nothingness" and learned personality (The Road To Me), then you are on the verge of remembering who you truly are.

Then and only then can you walk with intentioned abundance.